My Shared Readings

Table of Contents

Being a Good Community Member

Many Kinds of Characters

Plants and Animals Grow and Change

Stories Have a Narrator

Technology at Work

Katie's Crop

Katie wanted to help people. She had an idea. She planted a tiny plant and took good care of it. It grew into a huge cabbage! When she gave it away, it helped feed a lot of people. Now other kids are growing food to give away, too.

Kind Hearts Are Gardens

by Henry Wadsworth Longfellow

Kind hearts are the gardens,
Kind thoughts are the roots,
Kind words are the flowers,
Kind deeds are the fruits.

Save Our Planet

It is our job to keep Earth clean. This girl saw litter on the ground, so she picked it up. You can help, too. Put trash where it belongs. Recycle cans and paper. If your old toys are still good, give them away. Then other kids can play with them.

What Will Max Do?

Max really wants a snack, but he does not have enough money. Is that a dollar on the floor? Max picks it up. Now he can get a snack! What will he get?

"Oh, no!" he hears Ana cry. Max knows what to do.

"This must be yours," he says.

Jim Henson

Do you know who Jim Henson was? Maybe not. But you know the puppets he created. Kermit the Frog is one, and Miss Piggy is another. Kids all over the world love Jim Henson's Muppets.

The More We Work Together

The more we work together,

Together, together,

The more we work together,

The happier we'll be.

For your work is my work,

And my work is your work.

The more we work together,

The happier we'll be.

A Pet for Meg

Meg wanted a pet. Dad said, "Let's go to the shelter!"

They looked at lots of cute pets. Then Meg saw Pixie. Pixie had big pointy ears. Her fur was a mess and her tongue stuck out!

"Who would take *this* dog?" asked Dad.

"I will!" said Meg. And she did!

Read to Me

by Jane Yolen

Read to me riddles
and read to me rhymes,
read to me stories
of magical times.
Read to me tales
about castles and kings,
read to me stories
of fabulous things.
Read to me pirates,
and read to me knights,
read to me dragons
and dragon-back flights.
Read to me spaceships
and cowboys and then
when you are finished—
please read them again!

Nan and Blue

All of Nan's crayons were happy, but not Blue. Blue felt very blue.

"I will run away," he said. He rolled under the bed to hide. Now Nan was blue, too. Her pictures were all wrong without Blue. When Nan found Blue, she cried, "My favorite color!" Nan was happy—and Blue was, too.

The Tortoise and the Hare

Hare always bragged about how fast he could run. He teased Tortoise for being slow.

One day Tortoise said, "Let's race!" Hare took off!

He bragged, "I'll take a nap and still win!"

Tortoise passed Hare and kept going—slow and steady. Tortoise won! Hare never bragged again.

A Smart Hen

Each morning Penny woke up Max. The hen flapped up to Max's window and pecked. She wanted breakfast! Every day, Max said, "It's too early!"

Penny was smart, but Max was smarter.

He put a cob of corn on a string and hung it outside his window. Penny got her breakfast. Max got his sleep!

Chums

by Arthur Guiterman

He sits and begs, he gives a paw.

He is, as you can see,

The finest dog you ever saw,

And he belongs to me.

He follows everywhere I go

And even when I swim.

I laugh because he thinks, you know,

That I belong to him.

The Amazing Butterfly

First a butterfly laid a tiny egg on a leaf. Then the egg hatched. A little caterpillar crawled out. The caterpillar ate and ate.

It crunched on plants. The caterpillar grew. Next it made itself a case. The caterpillar changed inside the case. At last, out came a butterfly!

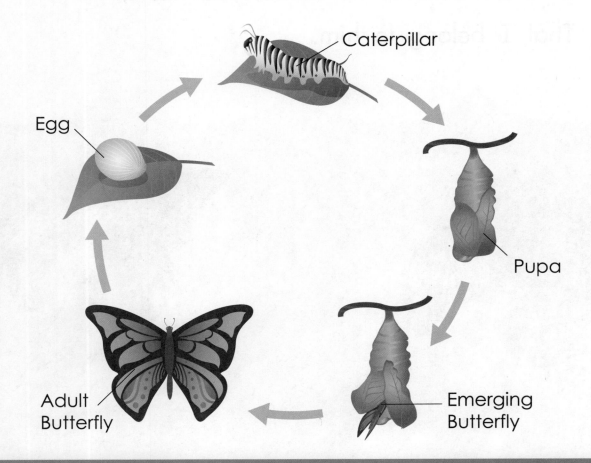

Caterpillar

Egg

Pupa

Adult
Butterfly

Emerging
Butterfly

16

Caterpillar

by Christina Rossetti

Brown and furry

Caterpillar in a hurry,

Take your walk

To the shady leaf, or stalk,

Or what not,

Which may be the chosen spot.

No toad spy you,

Hovering bird of prey pass by you;

Spin and die,

To live again a butterfly.

An Apple Grows

In the center of an apple, there are seeds. Those seeds can grow into apple trees. Flowers bloom on apple trees every spring.

After a while, the flowers fall off. In the spot where each flower was, an apple starts to grow. The apples are big and ripe in the fall. Then it's time to pick them.

Sunflower

Sunflower, sunflower,
Standing straight and tall,
Sunflower, sunflower,
You're the tallest flower
of them all!
Sunflower, sunflower,
When your seeds fall
to the ground,
Sunflower, sunflower,
By the squirrels they'll
be found!

A Tree for Sam

"Let's plant a tree!" says Mom.

Sam is excited. "I've always wanted a tree to climb."

When Mom brings home the tree, Sam says, "That's it? It's so small!"

"Don't worry," Mom says. "It will grow, just like you. It will be big enough to climb in a few years."

Welcome, Ducklings!

Ducklings can walk when they are just one day old. They know how to swim, too. The mother duck keeps her ducklings together, so they will be safe. She teaches them how to find food. Ducklings find bugs and plants to eat in and by the water.

When ducklings are two months old, they are able to fly. When it gets cold, they fly to a warmer place.

Home Sweet Home

Do you know the yellow house?
I live there. Maybe you have seen
me napping on the step. Or you
may have seen me out walking. I don't
go too far. When my lady misses me,
she calls, "Here, kitty!"

My name is not kitty! I will not come!
But now it's dark and cold, so I slink
home. I yowl and she opens the door.

"Tank!" she cries. "Where were you?"
It's good to be home.

Good Neighbors

by May Justus

A little old woman
   and a little old mouse
Live in the very same
   little old house.
She rocks in a corner,
He scampers in the wall,
And they never, never get
   in each other's way at all.

A Big Fish?

"Come on, Jen," says Chip. "I feel lucky. Let's go catch some fish!"

Jen gets her rod and runs after Chip. They sit on the dock with their rods in the water. Something tugs on Chip's line!

Chip says, "I think I've caught a big one!"

He pulls up his line. It's not a big fish. It's a soggy, blue mitten!

"I've been looking for that mitten!" laughs Chip.

My Mom, the Vet

My mom loves animals. She is a vet. A vet is a doctor for animals. Vets help animals when they get sick. They help animals stay healthy, too.

Some vets take care of farm animals and zoo animals. My mom works in a clinic. She takes care of dogs, cats, and other pets. I love to visit my mom at work. One day, I want to be a vet, too!

The Kickball Game

I can hear the bell ring. It's time for recess. I have to get ready. Here they come!

I see the kids running. A boy picks me up and yells, "Who wants to play kickball?"

They all scream, "I do! I do!"

A girl takes her turn. Here comes the kick. *Ouch*! She is really strong! When will this game end? *Brrrring*! Recess is over. Ah, I can rest until lunchtime.

I Had a Little Hen

I had a little hen, the prettiest ever seen,
She washed up the dishes
    and kept the house clean.
She went to the mill to fetch me some flour,
And brought it home in less than an hour.
She baked me my bread,
She fetched me my mail,
She sat by the fire and told a fine tale!

Carrier Pigeons

Did you know that some birds take messages to people? These birds are called carrier pigeons. People train the birds. They strap a tiny message to the bird's leg. Then the bird takes the message to the right place.

Many people used carrier pigeons long ago—before they had radios, phones, and computers. Today, people raise carrier pigeons as a hobby.

Atom's Day Off

Data left for her job. Atom did all the chores in the house. He washed, cooked, and cleaned. Data knew Atom was tired of working so hard.

That day, Atom took a break. He lost track of time. *Oh, no!* There was no supper ready. "Sorry!" Atom beeped.

"It's OK," beeped Data. "I brought Bolt Burgers as a treat."

"Yum!" beeped Atom. "Thanks!"

A Handy Machine

Some schools have a special way to make sure all the kids can get lunch. They don't need money or lunch cards. They just have to scan their hands to pay for their lunches. How does it work? No one has the same handprint as anyone else. The scanner can "read" a hand and know who it is. It's like having a built-in code!

Two Places at Once

Ms. Ruiz was stuck in traffic. "I'll never get to school on time," she said.

She had planned to finish reading her class a book that day. They couldn't wait to find out the ending. She pulled over to a safe place and called Mr. Jones, the substitute.

"What a great idea!" he said as he put his phone on speaker. "Listen up, kids."

Ms. Ruiz set up her tablet and began reading to the class. Who says you can't be in two places at the same time?

Unplug!

It's fun to watch TV and play games online. However, one group of people thought they were spending too much time looking at screens. These people decided to take a break from technology.

One day each week, they do not use cell phones or computers, or watch TV. You can try it, too. There is plenty to do when you unplug. You can read, build things, or dance. Go outside. Ride your bike, jump rope, or watch clouds drift by. You may find out that being unplugged is fun, too!

I Wonder

I wonder who invented *A*
and who invented *B*
and all the other letters
from *C* to *P* to *Z*.

I wonder if they knew back then
that we'd have books and things
like e-mail and text messages
to give those letters wings.

I wonder if they knew back then
the word T-E-C-H-N-O-L-O-G-Y
and how their ABCs would change
the world for kids like me.

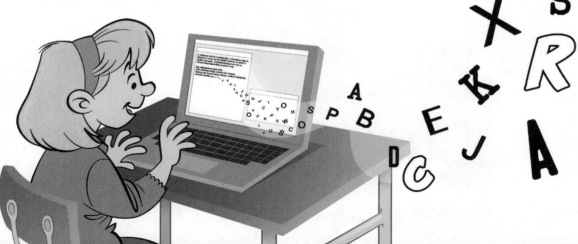

Not So Scary

Pony lives on the farm. Pony likes the chickens. They are nice. Pony loves to dance with the funny goats, too. What does Pony NOT like? The large, scary cow.

One day, Pony goes outside to find Mama. Where can Mama be? Poor Pony is about to cry when a gentle voice says, "Look over there, Pony."

It is the cow! She's not so scary after all.

The Strongest Things

by *Constance Andrea Keremes*

A tubby tugboat looks just like
    A toy to you and me.
But it is strong enough to pull
    A big ship out to sea.

A little ant no bigger than
    A spot upon the floor,
Can carry crumbs ten times his weight
    Quite easily through the door.
I guess it goes to show you
    That size matters not at all.
Some of the strongest things I see
    Are really very small.

Pete Saves the Day

Pete hopped on his bike and rode to the park. The big kids were playing ball.

"Can I play?" Pete asked.

Gus said, "You are too small."

Pete sighed and sat to watch Gus bat. Gus hit the ball hard. *CRACK!* It rolled under a bush with huge, long thorns.

"These thorns are sharp, and my hand is too big," Gus said.

Pete said, "I can get it!" He put his small hand in. Got it!

Dog and His Bone

Dog holds a big bone as he trots by the stream. What does Dog see when he looks in the water? He sees a dog with a big bone! Dog wants that bone.

It looks even better than the one he has. Dog growls, but the other dog growls back. Dog REALLY wants that bone, so he barks. *Ker-plop!* Dog's bone falls into the water and sinks. Now Dog has no bone at all.

Why Bear Has a Short Tail

One day, Bear asked Fox how to catch many fish. Fox said, "Use your tail. Put it through the ice and fish will come and bite it."

So Bear made a hole in the ice and stuck his long, brown tail in the cold water. He waited and waited, but no fish came. Bear wanted to go home. Oh, no! His tail was frozen in the ice. He pulled until *pop*! Bear had only a short tail.

Jemma Jay

Jemma Jay will only eat plain bugs.
Mama begs, "Try some with spots."
Papa pleads, "Try some with stripes."
"No," Jemma says.
"Only plain bugs for me."

One day, there are no plain bugs.
Jemma is hungry. She is VERY hungry.
She takes a bite of a spotty bug.
Mmm! It's not bad. In fact, it's good!
The striped one is tasty, too.
"Yum! All bugs for me!" says Jemma.

The First Cars

Out on the road today, there are lots of cars. That was not always the case. The first car was made in 1769, but cars were not popular until the early 1900s.

In 1908, Henry Ford began making a car called a Model T. Ford's workers made Model Ts until 1927. Unlike cars today, the Model T was slow and kind of plain. But the Model T did not cost much and it worked well. It changed the way people lived!

Horses to the Rescue

Tom groaned. He had not seen the hole in the road. When the front wheel of the car hit it, the car bounced. It went right into the pond! How was he going to get it out?

Just then, Tom heard a laugh. Mr. Shay and his team of horses looked over the fence. "Need help?" Mr. Shay asked. He tossed Tom a rope to tie to the car. The horses pulled the car out.

"Give me a horse any day," Mr. Shay said. On this day, Tom had to agree!

The U.S. in Space

In 1961, Alan Shepard became the first American to go into space. His flight did not go all the way around Earth. A year later, in February 1962, John Glenn orbited Earth three times. In July 1969, a team of U.S. astronauts landed on the moon.

Today, there are rovers showing us pictures of Mars. Maybe one day astronauts will land on Mars.

But Children Had Fun Anyway

by Constance Andrea Keremes

Two hundred years ago or more,

You could not buy toys in a store.

Not one computer game to play,

But children had fun anyway.

Boys and girls would play pretend,

And hide-and-seek games with a friend.

They often made their own toys too,

From sacks and stones—a stick or two.

A doll, a ball, a rolling hoop,

A stick horse, pail, and little scoop.

Not one computer game to play,

But children had fun anyway.

The Washington Monument

The Washington Monument is a white, pointy tower that reaches high into the sky. It is located in our country's capital, Washington, D.C.

The tower was built to honor George Washington. It opened in 1889. It's as tall as a 50-story building and has 897 steps. But people don't have to climb to get to the top. It has an elevator, too. Thousands of people visit the monument each year.

An Amazing Sight

Lee had always wanted to visit Mount Rushmore, and here he was. He stared at the four huge heads of the presidents. It was hard to believe they were carved right into the mountain.

"Dad," Lee said, "did you know that each head is as tall as a six-story building? The noses are 20 feet long!"

"Wow," said Dad. "I wonder what would happen if they sneezed!" Lee laughed. He thought he saw George Washington wink and smile, too!

A Star Party

"It's dark! Can we start?" Karla asked. Karla was having a star party with her friends at the farm. They would look at stars through Mom's telescope.

"Yes, let's go," Mom said.

Outside, far away from city lights, Karla and her friends looked at the sky. They saw many stars. Then they looked through the telescope. One star was big and bright! Mom told them it was a planet, not a star. It was Mars.

"Let's call it a sky party!" Karla said.

On Mars

Mars is millions of miles away from us. We know what the surface of the planet looks like. A kind of robot called a rover is on Mars now. It is sending pictures and information back to scientists on Earth.

The rover is a machine, but in some ways it seems alive. It can move. It has "eyes" that are cameras and an arm that can pick up rocks. The rover's body holds many important parts, and its brain is a computer.

It's a Comet!

A comet is a large chunk of ice and dust that orbits, or goes around, the sun. It is like a big, dirty snowball. Comets travel far out into the solar system and then move back toward the sun.

A comet has a main core called a nucleus. The nucleus is made of ice, dust, gas, and rock. It can be several miles wide. When a comet gets close to the sun, some of the dust and gas form a long, glowing tail.

The Moon's the North Wind's Cookie

by Vachel Lindsay

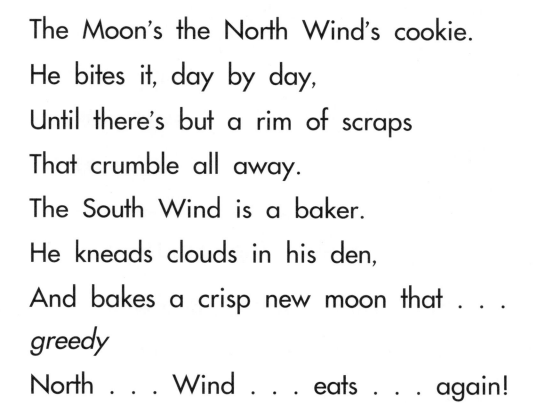

The Moon's the North Wind's cookie.

He bites it, day by day,

Until there's but a rim of scraps

That crumble all away.

The South Wind is a baker.

He kneads clouds in his den,

And bakes a crisp new moon that . . .
greedy
North . . . Wind . . . eats . . . again!

49

Shapes in the Clouds

Sam dropped the ball near Mom and frowned. "Kurt didn't come. Can we go home?" Sam asked.

Mom said, "Okay. But first, let's look at the clouds."

Sam nodded and sat down. He liked finding shapes in the clouds.

"I see a bird," Mom said. Sam saw it, too. The cloud looked like it had wings.

"I see a boat with two oars," Sam said. "And now it's turning into a race car!" Sam smiled. He felt better. This was just as much fun as football.

The Sun

The sun is a star—a huge, hot, shining ball of gases. Earth and the other planets in our solar system orbit around the sun. The sun is very important. Without it, there would be no life on Earth.

Living creatures on Earth depend on energy from the sun. We need the heat and the light. Plants use sunlight to make food. Then they grow and give off oxygen. People and animals breathe the oxygen and eat the plants.

Almond Milk

Many people drink and enjoy cows' milk. However, some people can't drink dairy milk. They drink almond milk instead. Almond milk is good for you, and some people think it tastes even better than cows' milk.

You can buy almond milk, but making it at home is easy. First, soak raw almonds in water. Then, pour the water off. Blend the nuts with fresh water until the mixture is smooth. Add vanilla, if you like.

A Farmer's Boy

Anonymous

We walked in the lane together;

The sky was covered with stars.

We reached the gate in silence

As I lifted down the bars.

She neither smiled nor thanked me

Because she knew not how

For I was only a Farmer's Boy

And she was a Jersey Cow.

Animal Dentists

It's important for people to get their teeth checked. People aren't the only ones who need dentists. Animals do, too. However, animal dentists can't tell their patients, "Open wide!"

Many animals dislike having their teeth cleaned or fixed. An animal can be dangerous, too. Just think of a lion's pointy teeth! So how can the dentist clean or fix an animal's teeth? The dentist uses medicine to make the animal sleep until the job is done.

Double Trouble

Jack and Jeff did not want to go see Dr. Vega. The dentist was nice, but Jack didn't like the noisy machine she used to clean his teeth. Jeff didn't like looking up into the bright light.

When the boys got to the office, Dr. Vega had a surprise for them. She gave Jack a pair of headphones. He got to listen to music, not the machine!

She gave Jeff a pair of sunglasses so the light would not bother him. Going to the dentist was not a problem now.

Field Trip Funds

Mr. Soto's class was planning a trip to the zoo. They needed to earn money to pay for the trip. Some kids wanted to have a book sale at school. They could sell their old books. A book sale would be pretty easy.

Other kids wanted to walk dogs to make money. They knew lots of people in the neighborhood who had dogs. Walking dogs sounded like a job everyone would enjoy. The class voted, and the dogs won!

A New Kind of Eggs

My family and I are vegetarians. We don't eat meat, fish, or eggs. Today, though, I ate bread with a new kind of eggs. They weren't chicken eggs. They were an egg substitute made from plants!

Plant eggs are made from peas and beans. They're great for people who don't or can't eat eggs from chickens. In bread, you can't tell the difference between a chicken egg and a plant egg. I think plant eggs are a cool invention!

Dogs Help the Deaf

Some sounds, like a beeping car, warn you to watch out. Some people may not hear those sounds, because they are deaf. A furry friend called a "hearing dog" can help them.

The dog learns to turn and look at something it hears, like a horn or a siren. Then its owner turns to look, too. The dog helps keep its owner safe. At home, the dog lets a person know when the doorbell rings or the baby cries. Hearing dogs are helpful pals!

I Know All the Sounds That the Animals Make

by Jack Prelutsky

I know all the sounds
   that the animals make,
and make them all day from
   the moment I wake,
I roar like a mouse and
   I purr like a moose,
I hoot like a duck and
   I moo like a goose.
I squeak like a cat and
   I quack like a frog,
I oink like a bear and I
   honk like a hog,
I croak like a cow and
   I bark like a bee,

no wonder the animals marvel at me.

59

Rainbow

Hard rain falls, I'm stuck inside.

I'd rather get my bike and ride.

The clouds above make rain below.

I know rain makes the flowers grow.

The sun peeks out and says to rain,

"It's time for me to shine again.

So move aside and let me through

And I'll put on a show for you."

The sun and raindrops have a fight.

Who will win—I hope the light!

The streets and puddles start to dry,

And then a rainbow paints the sky.

My Homemade Band

My older sister, Cam, is in a band.
Cam plays the drums. I want to play
her drums, but she won't let me.
"I'll make my own band," I said.
"Good idea," Cam said. "I'll help."
We got some jars, boxes, and bottles
from the recycling bin. Then I found
some rubber bands in the desk. Cam
saw a lot of good stuff in the kitchen.

When we were done, I called my friends.
"Want to play in my band?" I asked.
They did!

Day or Night?

What is the difference between day and night? In many places, the answer is simple! Day is light. Night is dark.

However, in some places near the North Pole, the answer is not so clear. One day each fall, the sun sets. Then it doesn't rise again for about eight weeks. It stays dark all day and all night! The opposite happens each spring. One day, the sun rises. It doesn't set for 11 weeks!

My Shadow

by Robert Louis Stevenson

I have a little shadow
that goes in and out with me,
And what can be the use of him
is more than I can see.
He is very, very like me
from the heels up to the head;
And I see him jump before me
when I jump into my bed.

Notes:

Notes:

Notes:

California Common Core State Standards for English Language Arts (CA CCSS)
California English Language Development Standards (CA ELD)

Flip Book

My Standards

Grade 1

Fold here

DIRECTIONS
for making the Flip Book:

1. Fold each page away from you along the dotted line. When the yellow cover is on top, the page you're now reading should be on the bottom.

1. Place the pages together so that the second page inserts into the first page, and the third inserts into the second page. Once your Flip Book is assembled, staple along the spine.

1. Flip through all the standards referring to the color-coded standards labels.

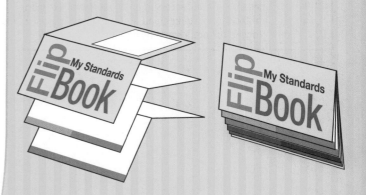

Dear Family Members,

This year, our Grade 1 students will continue their literacy journey using the **Benchmark Ready to Advance** program. Our reading, writing, listening, and speaking instruction will reflect the standards outlined in the **California Common Core State Standards for English Language Arts**. The goal of these standards is to prepare all of our students for the demands of college and careers. In addition, our instruction will support English learners to meet all of the **California English Language Development Standards**.

This flip book summarizes the standards our Grade 1 students will learn and practice in each unit of the program. Family communications for each unit will provide you with the standards being taught in that unit plus ideas and activities to help you support students applying and mastering those standards.

We look forward to an exciting year of literacy growth!

CA CCSS **Reading Standards for Literature**	Units									
	1	2	3	4	5	6	7	8	9	10
RL.1.1 Ask and answer questions about key details in a text.										
RL.1.2 Retell stories, including key details, and demonstrate understanding of their central message or lesson.										
RL.1.3 Describe characters, settings, and major events in a story, using key details.										
RL.1.4 Identify words and phrases in stories or poems that suggest feelings or appeal to the senses. **(See grade 1 Language standards 4–6 for additional expectations.) CA**										
RL.1.5 Explain major differences between books that tell stories and books that give information, drawing on a wide reading of a range of text types.										
RL.1.6 Identify who is telling the story at various points in a text.										
RL.1.7 Use illustrations and details in a story to describe its characters, setting, or events.										
RL.1.9 Compare and contrast the adventures and experiences of characters in stories.										
RL.1.10 10. With prompting and support, read prose and poetry of appropriate complexity for grade 1. **a. Activate prior knowledge related to the information and events in a text. CA** **b. Confirm predictions about what will happen next in a text. CA**										

CA ELD Part II: Learning About How English Works	Units									
	1	2	3	4	5	6	7	8	9	10
ELD.PII.1.1 Understanding text structure										
ELD.PII.1.2 Understanding cohesion										
ELD.PII.1.3 Using verbs and verb phrases										
ELD.PII.1.4 Using nouns and noun phrases										
ELD.PII.1.5 Modifying to add details										
ELD.PII.1.6 Connecting ideas										
ELD.PII.1.7 Condensing ideas										

CA ELD Part III: Using Foundational Literacy Skills	Units									
	1	2	3	4	5	6	7	8	9	10
ELD.PIII.1.1 The California English Language Development Standards correspond to California's Common Core State Standards for English Language Arts (ELA). English learners should have full access to and opportunities to learn ELA, mathematics, science, history/social studies, and other content at the same time they are progressing toward full proficiency in English.										

CA CCSS Reading Standards for Informational Text

	Units									
	1	2	3	4	5	6	7	8	9	10
RI.1.1 Ask and answer questions about key details in a text.										
RI.1.2 Identify the main topic and retell key details of a text.										
RI.1.3 Describe the connection between two individuals, events, ideas, or pieces of information in a text.										
RI.1.4 Ask and answer questions to help determine or clarify the meaning of words and phrases in a text. (See grade 1 Language standards 4–6 for additional expectations.) CA										
RI.1.5 Know and use various text **structures** (e.g., **sequence**) and **text** features (e.g., headings, tables of contents, glossaries, electronic menus, icons) to locate key facts or information in a text. CA										
RI.1.6 Distinguish between information provided by pictures or other illustrations and information provided by the words in a text.										
RI.1.7 Use the illustrations and details in a text to describe its key ideas.										
RI.1.8 Identify the reasons an author gives to support points in a text.										
RI.1.9 Identify basic similarities in and differences between two texts on the same topic (e.g., in illustrations, descriptions, or procedures).										
RI.1.10 With prompting and support, read informational texts appropriately complex for grade 1. a. **Activate prior knowledge** related to the information and events in a text. CA b. **Confirm predictions** about what will happen next in a text. CA										

Fold here

CA ELD Part I: Interacting in Meaningful Ways

	Units									
	1	2	3	4	5	6	7	8	9	10
ELD.PI.1.1 Exchanging information and ideas with others through oral collaborative conversations on a range of social and academic topics										
ELD.PI.1.2 Interacting with others in written English in various communicative forms (print, communicative technology, and multimedia)										
ELD.PI.1.3 Offering and supporting opinions and negotiating with others in communicative exchanges										
ELD.PI.1.4 Adapting language choices to various contexts (based on task, purpose, audience, and text type)										
ELD.PI.1.5 Listening actively to spoken English in a range of social and academic contexts										
ELD.PI.1.6 Reading closely literary and informational texts and viewing multimedia to determine how meaning is conveyed explicitly and implicitly through language										
ELD.PI.1.7 Evaluating how well writers and speakers use language to support ideas and opinions with details or reasons depending on modality, text type, purpose, audience, topic, and content area										
ELD.PI.1.8 Analyzing how writers and speakers use vocabulary and other language resources for specific purposes (to explain, persuade, entertain, etc.) depending on modality, text type, purpose, audience, topic, and content area										
ELD.PI.1.9 Expressing information and ideas in formal oral presentations on academic topics										
ELD.PI.1.10 Writing literary and informational texts to present, describe, and explain ideas and information, using appropriate technology										
ELD.PI.1.11 Supporting own opinions and evaluating others' opinions in speaking and writing										
ELD.PI.1.12 Selecting and applying varied and precise vocabulary and language structures to effectively convey ideas										

CA CCSS **Reading Standards for Foundational Skills**		Units									
		1	2	3	4	5	6	7	8	9	10
RF.1.1	Demonstrate understanding of the organization and basic features of print. a. Recognize the distinguishing features of a sentence (e.g., first word, capitalization, ending punctuation).										
RF.1.2	Demonstrate understanding of spoken words, syllables, and sounds (phonemes). a. Distinguish long from short vowel sounds in spoken single-syllable words. b. Orally produce single-syllable words by blending sounds (phonemes), including consonant blends. c. Isolate and pronounce initial, medial vowel, and final sounds (phonemes) in spoken single-syllable words. d. Segment spoken single-syllable words into their complete sequence of individual sounds (phonemes).										
RF.1.3	Know and apply grade-level phonics and word analysis skills in decoding words **both in isolation and in text. CA** a. Know the spelling-sound correspondences for common consonant digraphs. b. Decode regularly spelled one-syllable words. c. Know final -e and common vowel team conventions for representing long vowel sounds. d. Use knowledge that every syllable must have a vowel sound to determine the number of syllables in a printed word. e. Decode two-syllable words following basic patterns by breaking the words into syllables. f. Read words with inflectional endings. g. Recognize and read grade-appropriate irregularly spelled words.										

L.1.5	With guidance and support from adults, demonstrate understanding of word relationships and nuances in word meanings. a. Sort words into categories (e.g., colors, clothing) to gain a sense of the concepts the categories represent. b. Define words by category and by one or more key attributes (e.g., a *duck* is a bird that swims; a *tiger* is a large cat with stripes). c. Identify real-life connections between words and their use (e.g., note places at home that are *cozy*). d. Distinguish shades of meaning among verbs differing in manner (e.g., *look, peek, glance, stare, glare, scowl*) and adjectives differing in intensity (e.g., *large, gigantic*) by defining or choosing them or by acting out the meanings.										
L.1.6	Use words and phrases acquired through conversations, reading and being read to, and responding to texts, including using frequently occurring conjunctions to signal simple relationships (e.g., *because*).										

CA CCSS **Language Standards**	Units									
	1	2	3	4	5	6	7	8	9	10
L.1.1 Demonstrate command of the conventions of standard English grammar and usage when writing or speaking. a. Print all upper- and lowercase letters. b. Use common, proper, and possessive nouns. c. Use singular and plural nouns with matching verbs in basic sentences (e.g., *He hops; We hop*). d. Use personal **(subject, object)**, possessive, and indefinite pronouns (e.g., *I, me, my; they, them, their; anyone, everything*). **CA** e. Use verbs to convey a sense of past, present, and future (e.g., *Yesterday I walked home; Today I walk home; Tomorrow I will walk home*). f. Use frequently occurring adjectives. g. Use frequently occurring conjunctions (e.g., *and, but, or, so, because*). h. Use determiners (e.g., articles, demonstratives). i. Use frequently occurring prepositions (e.g., *during, beyond, toward*). j. Produce and expand complete simple and compound declarative, interrogative, imperative, and exclamatory sentences in response to prompts.										
L.1.2 2. Demonstrate command of the conventions of standard English capitalization, punctuation, and spelling when writing. a. Capitalize dates and names of people. b. Use end punctuation for sentences. c. Use commas in dates and to separate single words in a series. d. Use conventional spelling for words with common spelling patterns and for frequently occurring irregular words. e. Spell untaught words phonetically, drawing on phonemic awareness and spelling conventions.										
L.1.4 Determine or clarify the meaning of unknown and multiple-meaning words and phrases based on *grade 1 reading and content,* choosing flexibly from an array of strategies. a. Use sentence-level context as a clue to the meaning of a word or phrase. b. Use frequently occurring affixes as a clue to the meaning of a word. c. Identify frequently occurring root words (e.g., *look*) and their inflectional forms (e.g., *looks, looked, looking*).										

Fold here

CA CCSS **Writing Standards**	Units									
	1	2	3	4	5	6	7	8	9	10
W.1.1	Write opinion pieces in which they introduce the topic or name the book they are writing about, state an opinion, supply a reason for the opinion, and provide some sense of closure.									
W.1.2	Write informative/explanatory texts in which they name a topic, supply some facts about the topic, and provide some sense of closure.									
W.1.3	Write narratives in which they recount two or more appropriately sequenced events, include some details regarding what happened, use temporal words to signal event order, and provide some sense of closure.									
W.1.5	With guidance and support from adults, focus on a topic, respond to questions and suggestions from peers, and add details to strengthen writing as needed.									
W.1.6	With guidance and support from adults, use a variety of digital tools to produce and publish writing, including in collaboration with peers.									
W.1.7	Participate in shared research and writing projects (e.g., explore a number of "how-to" books on a given topic and use them to write a sequence of instructions).									
W.1.8	With guidance and support from adults, recall information from experiences or gather information from provided sources to answer a question.									

CA CCSS **Speaking and Listening Standards**	Units									
	1	2	3	4	5	6	7	8	9	10
SL.1.1	Participate in collaborative conversations with diverse partners about *grade 1 topics and texts* with peers and adults in small and larger groups. a. Follow agreed-upon rules for discussions (e.g., listening to others with care, speaking one at a time about the topics and texts under discussion). b. Build on others' talk in conversations by responding to the comments of others through multiple exchanges. c. Ask questions to clear up any confusion about the topics and texts under discussion.									
SL.1.2	Ask and answer questions about key details in a text read aloud or information presented orally or through other media. **a. Give, restate, and follow simple two-step directions. CA**									
SL.1.3	Ask and answer questions about what a speaker says in order to gather additional information or clarify something that is not understood.									
SL.1.4	Describe people, places, things, and events with relevant details, expressing ideas and feelings clearly. **a. Memorize and recite poems, rhymes, and songs with expression. CA**									
SL.1.5	Add drawings or other visual displays to descriptions when appropriate to clarify ideas, thoughts, and feelings.									
SL.1.6	Produce complete sentences when appropriate to task and situation. (See grade 1 Language standards 1 and 3 for specific expectations.)									